Floella's Fabulous Bright Ideas Book

Are you ready to have fun
and laughs?
Are you keen to play tricks on
your friends and surprise them?
Then read on, because Floella has
heaps of bright ideas for *you* to
try out!

Illustrated by Chris Evans

*Also by Floella Benjamin
in Magnet Books*

Floella's Fun Book

Floella's FABULOUS BRIGHT IDEAS BOOK

Floella Benjamin

A Magnet Book

For Aston

First published in 1986 as a Magnet paperback by
Methuen Children's Books Ltd
11 New Fetter Lane, London EC4P 4EE
Text copyright © 1986 Floella Benjamin
Illustrations copyright © 1986 Chris Evans
Printed in Great Britain

ISBN 0 416 52880 5

Hi there! Floella here.

Are you ready to have fun and laughs?

Are you keen to play tricks on your friends and to surprise them?

Well, I hope you are, because I have thought up for you 101 ways to do just that.

Indoors or outdoors, there are ways for you to enjoy yourselves. You can find out just who is a wally with my 'Clever Clogs' section, and who is game for a laugh in the 'Games' section. My favourite game is 'Tongue Tied'. That's what happens to you when you try to touch your nose with your tongue! (Go on try it . . . see what I mean.)

Hey, why not venture into the past or the future by becoming a knight in armour rescuing a damsel in distress, or be an astronaut meeting aliens in space.

I'll show you ways to have fun celebrating other nations' festivals, and how to throw parties with a difference. If you work up an appetite with all the activities then try some of my yummy 'Scrummy Tucks'. It all adds up to 101 ways of having fun!

Well, that's enough talking for now, let's get down to it!

Have fun,
Floella.

STAR SIGNS

I love talking to people and finding out about them.
Something I always ask the people I meet is "When were you born?" Then I know what star sign they are.

Libra
I was born on 23rd of September. That means my star sign is 'Libra'. Anyone born between 23rd September and 22nd October comes under the sign of Libra, the Scales.

We Librans are meant to be peace loving, fair minded people who like tasteful surroundings. Our lucky day is meant to be Friday. What sign of the Zodiac are you? . . . Let me guess.

Aries
Are you an Aries the Ram? You are if you were born between 21st March and 20th April. Arians are meant to be energetic people who love exploring new places and organising people. Their lucky day is said to be Tuesday.

Taurus
Or were you born under the sign of Taurus the Bull? 21st April to 21st May. If so, you may be kind and practical with a bit of a stubborn streak. Your lucky day is Friday.

Gemini

Don't tell me, you're a Gemini, the sign of the Twins, and you were born between 22nd May and 21st June! Do you know you are meant to be quick-minded types who love reading, writing, talking and trying to do two things at the same time? Your lucky day is Wednesday.

Cancer

Now if you were born between 22nd June and 23rd July then Cancer the Crab is your sign. You might be a determined, adaptable, homeloving person whose special day is Monday.

Leo

Leo the Lion is your sign if you were born between 24th July and 23rd August. Leos like to be leaders and love being the centre of attention. They make good kings or queens and Leos' special day is Sunday.

Virgo

Are you a perfectionist? Do you like everything to be neat and tidy? Well that is what they say about Virgo people. They are born between 24th August and 22nd September and their day is Wednesday.

7

Scorpio

Scorpio the Scorpion is your sign if you were born between 23rd October and 22nd November. Do you always say what you think and enjoy solving mysteries? Well, that's what Scorpio people are supposed to be like and their special day is Tuesday.

Sagittarius

If you're born between 23rd November and 21st December your sign is Sagittarius, the Archer. You're supposed to be adventurous, fun loving people who enjoy travelling. Your day is Thursday.

Capricorn

Capricorn, the Goat, is your sign if you were born between 22nd December and 20th January. You can be clever, without really trying, and you love your home. Capricorn's day is Tuesday.

Aquarius

Aquarius, the Water Carrier, is one of my favourite signs. You belong to this sign if you were born between 21st January and 19th February. The reason I love Aquarians is because I find them so much fun to be with. They are usually very kind and friendly. Their special day is Saturday.

Pisces

Pisces, the Fish, is your sign if you were born between 20th February and 20th March. Some say that Pisceans are great day dreamers. Your day is Thursday.

Why not find out what sign all your friends and family come under?

Make a Zodiac mobile showing the signs. To do this, just draw the signs on card, colour them and cut them out. Pierce tiny holes in them and tie different lengths of cotton to each one. Tape two wire coat hangers together to form a cross and hang the cut-outs on. Now hang up your Zodiac mobile and add to it when you make new friends who have different star signs.

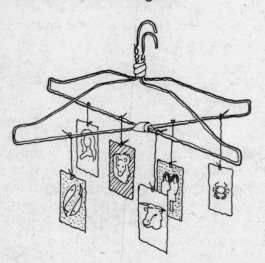

PUPPETS

Puppets can dance, Puppets can sing,
Puppets can really have a fling
When you bring them alive and do your thing.

So curtain up, light the lights
because there's no business like show puppet theatre
business. To start the action I'll show you how to make
three types of performing puppet.

Puppet on a stick

Draw some figures on a card, colour them and cut them
out. Alternatively, find figures in magazines, cut them
out and stick them on to card. Now attach the figures
to lengths of coat hanger wire.

You will need a theatre for the puppets to appear in, so this is what you do: Get a large box without a lid and cut a rectangle out of the front. In the middle of the two side panels cut out a slit. This is for your puppets to make their entrances through.

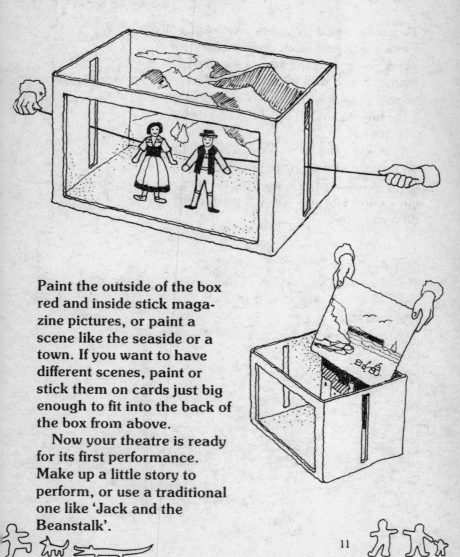

Paint the outside of the box red and inside stick magazine pictures, or paint a scene like the seaside or a town. If you want to have different scenes, paint or stick them on cards just big enough to fit into the back of the box from above.

Now your theatre is ready for its first performance. Make up a little story to perform, or use a traditional one like 'Jack and the Beanstalk'.

11

To make hand puppets use toilet rolls.
Paint them and stick pieces of felt for
eyes, noses and mouths. Use bits of
wool for hair and stick pieces of
material around them, as clothes. Put
your fingers inside the rolls to operate
the puppet.

    For your theatre use a table. Place it
on its side and operate your puppets
from behind. This is so that the audience can't see you. Why not try putting
on a musical!

Other sorts of puppets you can make
are **shadow puppets**. They can be great
fun, especially if they move. This is how you can get
them to do just that. Cut shapes of animals or people
out of card, cut the arms and legs separately and attach
them to the body with pipe cleaners, or split pins. Tape
wire or straws on to the back of the body and you will
be able to make them move.

To make the shadow theatre, use greaseproof paper
or a white sheet, and attach it with drawing pins to two
broomsticks supported by two chairs. You will need a
light behind you, so pull the curtains and use a table
lamp with the main room light turned off.

FESTIVALS

I love to find an excuse to celebrate, and festivals are a great reason to do so. Every country in the world has one or more festivals. In England we celebrate Christmas and Easter, to mention just a couple.

The **Chinese** celebrate Yuan Tan, their New Year. It's held at the end of January. Here's how you can celebrate with them:

Make yourself a Chinese dragon.

You need a kitchen roll tube, crepe paper, three long strips of thin card, glue, paint and a black felt pen. Paint the tube and leave it to dry. Cut around the middle of the tube leaving 4cm uncut and fold it in half and you have the dragon's head. Roll up two strips of card as the eyes and nose, and glue them into place. Curl the third strip of card over a pencil to make the dragon's tongue, and stick it inside the mouth with glue. Draw the teeth with a black felt-tip pen. Cut fringes at one end of the crepe paper and stick the other end around the dragon's head to make the body.

Use your finger to make the dragon snap . . . Argghhhh! . . .

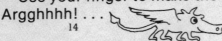

14

In **India** they celebrate Diwali (Festival of Light), when candles are lit and young ladies in beautiful saris dance and sing. **A sari** is one long piece of material and if you've never worn one, here's your chance. A two metre length of any light material will do, and this is how you wrap it.

You will need to wear a short blouse or tee shirt and a petticoat, then tuck one end of the material into the front of the petticoat and wind the sari once round your waist. Make three deep pleats and tuck the top of them into the petticoat. Wrap the fabric around the waist once more and put the rest of the material over your shoulder.

Now you're dressed to do your Indian dance.

In **America** children celebrate 'Trick or Treat' at Hallowe'en time. They run through the streets dressed as witches and ghosts, asking for goodies, and if they are not given any, they play tricks on people. You can join in the fun dressed as a witch. Here's **how to make a witch's hat:** You will need a circle of black paper about 45cm in diameter, a circle of thin black card or stiff paper about 35cm in diameter, tape and glue. Cut a straight line from the edge to the centre of the large circle. Bend it into a cone big enough to fit on your head, and stick it with tape. Mark out two circles on the

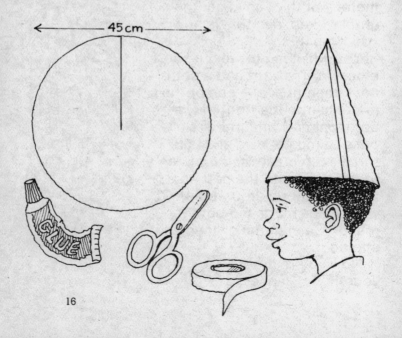

←———— 45 cm ————→

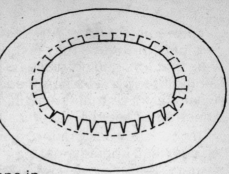

smaller piece of card, one inside the other. Make one about 6cm in diameter smaller than the bottom of the cone, and one the same size. Cut out the smaller circle and then cut lines in to the large circle to form tabs. Stick the brim of the hat to the cone with glue, and decorate with foil, stars and moons. Now you have a witch's hat.

All you need now is an old shawl to wrap round your shoulders and some green or purple face paint to make your face look horrible. (Use non-toxic powder paint mixed with baby lotion for this.) You're ready to be a witch! Remember to practise your shrieking witch's cackle . . .

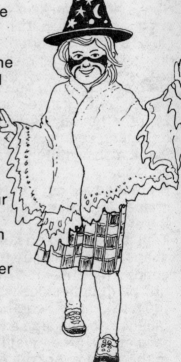

I really enjoy performing in the theatre, it's so exciting. In **Greece** they celebrate drama festivals where actors and actresses perform in huge open air theatres called amphitheatres. The performers wear masks so that the audience at the back of the theatre can see their expressions.

If you fancy performing, make yourself **a Greek tragedy and comedy mask**.

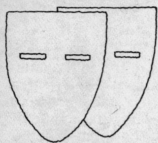

Here's what to do: You need two pieces of thick card about 15cm by 20cm, a thin stick or length of dowelling about 30cm long, white paint, a black felt-tip marker, glue and tape.

From the card cut out two mask shapes and cut out small slits for the eyes.

Tape the stick to one of the mask shapes and then glue the other shape firmly over it. When the glue is dry, paint both sides white. Now with the black marker carefully draw a tragic face on one side and a comical face on the other, just like the ones in the picture. Act out a scene holding the mask in front of your face. Turn it round when you want to change from sad to happy.

In **Japan** on the 3rd of March the girls celebrate 'Hina Matsuri', a doll festival. They make dolls out of paper and cloth, put them into straw baskets and float them on the rivers. They hope that the dolls end up in another world. Why not make a doll and float it away to another world?

This is what you do: You will need scissors, paper, tape and some coloured felt-tipped pens. Cut out the doll shape, as shown, from stiff paper and colour it in. Bend the legs and arms and fold back the flap so that the doll can sit up on its own. For the boat use an empty plastic container, colour it if you like. Tape the doll inside the boat using the flap. Now set it to sail in the bath.

SPACE ADVENTURE

5 . . . 4 . . . 3 . . . 2 . . . 1 Blast off into space.

You will need to put on your life support system and space helmet first.

For your life support system find a box a little narrower than your shoulders, and cut it into this shape. Tape two large plastic fizzy drinks bottles on to the back of the box. These are the oxygen cylinders.

For the helmet find a smaller box and cut a rectangular hole in the front like this. Now string 4 toilet roll tubes together and tape the end to one of the bottles, making sure to tape the string as well. Cut a small

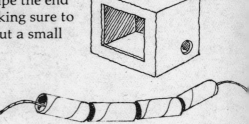

hole in the side of the helmet just big enough to wedge the other end of the toilet roll in. Secure it, and the string, with tape. This is your breathing tube. Pierce a small hole on top of the helmet and push in a drinking straw as a radio aerial.

To finish off the outfit, put on your wellington boots and see if you can find an old pair of rubber gloves to wear.

To blast off into space you'll need a **space shuttle**. To make one, use a box big enough to sit in. Cut off just the back flap; the side ones can be the wings and the front one is the control panel. Stick some bottle tops on to it as dials and knobs. Make two large holes at the back of the box and stick in two large plastic fizzy drinks bottles. These are your rocket engines.

Now you're ready to take off on your great space adventure.

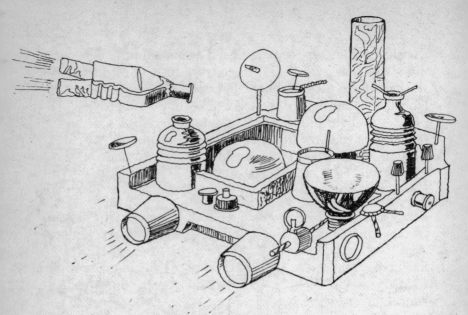

On your space travels you might come across a space
station or a flying saucer. **To make a space station**, use a
piece of polystyrene packing. This makes a good base.
Add towers made from kitchen roll tubes covered in foil,
yogurt pots and clear plastic bottles cut in half (the
bottom half could be used as a dome). All space stations
have radar scanners and you can make some out of plastic lids with cocktail sticks pushed through the middle and
then stuck into the polystyrene base.

   Now make radio contact with the space station.

COMMANDER FLOELLA REPORTING...

CALLING BASE, CALLING BASE...
COME IN PLEASE!... *

MAGIC TRICKS

Now, Ladies and Gentlemen, I would like to pass on to you a few magic tricks to impress your friends with. But first, every good magician needs a **Magic Wand**. To make a wand simply paint a 30cm stick black with white ends.

You will also need some magic words. I always use the magic words **"Hoko Poko, Fried fish and Coco!"** Now you can start the magic.

The first trick is the **Magic Wand Through The Glass Trick**. For this you'll need your magic wand and a clear plastic beaker or glass. Hold the glass up so that the audience can see it. Now take your magic wand, put it inside the glass and tap the bottom gently. Pull the wand out and repeat again. Now say the magic words, "Hoko Poko, Fried fish and Coco!"

This time push the wand between your hand and the glass until the end of the wand appears to go right through the bottom.

The next trick is the **Dry Handkerchief Trick** . . . Take an ordinary hanky and a beaker and a bowl of water. Push the hanky into the bottom of the beaker, then turn it upside down and put it in the bowl of water. Now say the magic words, "Hoko Poko, Fried fish and Coco!" . . . Take out the beaker, pull out the hanky and to everyone's surprise it's still dry!

Now for my next trick . . . The **Balancing Egg**. Take one ordinary egg and shake it vigorously. Before you put it down wave the magic wand over it and say the magic words . . . "Hoko Poko, Fried fish and Coco!" Now balance the egg on its end and it will stand up.

Next the **Floating Needle** . . . For this trick you will need a very ordinary needle which has been wiped with a thin layer of margerine. You will also need a small piece of blotting paper and a small bowl of water. Say to the audience "I will now make this needle float". Gently float the blotting paper on the water and carefully place the needle on it. Now, wave your magic wand slowly over the bowl saying the magic words . . . "Hoko Poko, Fried fish and Coco!" The blotting paper will slowly sink and the needle will be left floating on the surface.

Now for my **West Indian Rope Trick**. Take an ordinary piece of rope and show it to the audience. Let someone from the audience pull it to make sure there is nothing wrong with it, then ask him or her to tie a knot in it without letting go of the ends. Impossible! Now, lay it on the table and wave the magic wand over it saying the magic words . . . "Hoko Poko, Fried fish and Coco!" Fold your arms and pick up each end of the rope. Unfold your arms without letting go of the rope, pull . . . and there you have a knot in the middle. . . . Da da Dah.

Now for my **Drink Trick** . . . Place a plastic cup of water on a table. Announce that you will lift the glass from the table and drink the water without using your hands. Don't forget to wave the magic wand and say the magic words . . . "Hoko Poko, Fried fish and Coco!" Grip the cup between your teeth, tilt your head gently back and drink the water . . . "Look no hands!" . . . Da da dah!

Here's a **Magic Card Trick** . . . Take the three of
diamonds, the ace of hearts and the two of diamonds.
(Always hold them as illustrated.) Say to the
audience . . . "Observe the three of diamonds, the ace
of diamonds and the two of diamonds." Place the
cards face down on the table. Wave the magic wand
over the cards and say the magic words . . . "Hoko
Poko, Fried fish and Coco!" Now turn over the two
end cards one at a time and then finally the middle
one. The audience will be amazed to see the ace of
hearts has appeared . . . That's magic!

SHOPPING SPREE

Have a shopping spree in your own supermarket. Start by collecting as many empty food packets as you can, cereal packets, plastic bottles, egg boxes etc. Make sure they are all safe, of course; no glass bottles, bleach containers or sharp edges. Collect four medium-sized cardboard boxes to use as shelves, and two smaller ones to use as a basket and a till.

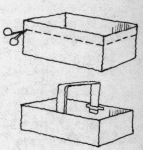

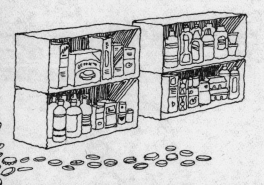

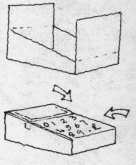

To make the basket simply cut the top two inches off the box and stick it together as shown in the picture.

Next, **for the shelves** trim the flaps off the boxes and stack them on top of each other. Paint them if you like, and secure them with tape to stop them falling over. Now fill up the shelves with the groceries.

For the check out, make a till out of a box. Cut it into the shape shown in the diagram and fold down the sides inwards and tape them together. Paint it and write the numbers 1 to 10 on the front. Use milk bottle tops as money. Have fun shopping and open your supermarket to your friends so they can do their shopping too.

Wally the delivery man has made a lot of mistakes today.
Can you help him make his deliveries to the right shops?

I went shopping and I bought a

I went shopping and I bought a

I went shopping and I bought a

I went shopping and I bought a

I went shopping and I bought a

I went shopping and I bought a

What have I left behind?

29

CLEVER CLOGS

I wonder how clever you are! Well here are a few brain teasers for you to sort out.

Jumbled Presents

What's inside the presents? Unscramble the words and find out.

DYTDE ARBE   ZPZUEL
LODL   CRA
COKERT   KASM
UCDK   MOCPUTRE

Teddy Bear, Doll, Rocket, Duck, Puzzle, Car, Mask, Computer.

Christmas Message

There's a Christmas message in the following code. What is it?

HIJKMNO . . . HIJKMNO . . .   Noel, Noel

Memory Matters

How good is your memory?
Well, have a look at the things on this page for fifteen seconds then close the book and try to remember all of them in thirty seconds.

Tongue Twisters

Now you've exercised your tongue, try saying these tricky
tongue twisters.

FLO'S FAB FROLICS. GOOD BLOOD, BAD BLOOD.
GREAT GREEK GRAPES. GROOVY GRAVY BABY.
RED LIP, YELLOW LIP.

Weird Words

Repeat these words as fast as you can to find out the
mystery words.
CHILLY-ACK. PEWTER-COM. CATPUSSY. PET-CAR.
WALLYIMA.

ACTUALLY, COMPUTER, PUSSYCAT, CARPET, I'M A WALLY.

KNIGHTS & CASTLES

Ever fancied being a prince or a princess living in a big castle? Well, here's your chance to have **your own castle**.

You will need some cardboard boxes, one large square one and two or three smaller ones. First cut the flaps off the large box, mark out the battlements and cut them out. Do the same with the windows. Next cut a drawbridge out of the side. Pierce holes at the corners of the drawbridge and two more through the wall either side. Thread two pieces of string through the holes and tie a knot in the ends. You can now pull the drawbridge up.

Stack and tape the smaller boxes to make a tall tower. Cut out some battlements and windows, and place the tower inside the castle walls.

Paint the whole castle grey with a brick pattern. You can even paint ivy growing up the walls.

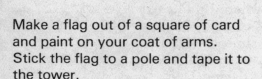

Make a flag out of a square of card
and paint on your coat of arms.
Stick the flag to a pole and tape it to
the tower.

Now you have a castle fit for a
prince or princess.

Use your castle to play 'damsels in
distress', 'knights in armour' or
'dungeons and dragons'.
Why not dress up as a damsel or a
knight?
To make a damsel's hat use a
large circle of card and roll it into a
cone shape. Tape it together and
stick some streamers on top.
For the knight's helmet use a
small box that fits over your head
and cut out a flap in one of the
sides. Make two or three slits in the
flap to see through.
For the plume, roll up some paper,
stick it with tape and make several
cuts down to half way on the roll.
Tape it to the top of the helmet.
Don't forget to give your castle
a name. You could name it after
yourself, your street or your
town, or make up a name like
'Castle Grim' or 'Merry Castle'.

TOWN AND COUNTRY

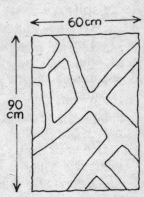

60cm

90 cm

I can never decide where I'd like to live best. Sometimes I enjoy being a town person, other times I wish I lived in the country or by the sea. You see, I just can't decide. Can you? I know! I'll make my own town and country places.

If you fancy a change too, **this is what to do:** Collect together as many small cardboard boxes as you can (cereal packets make good blocks of flats). Next, find a large sheet of plain paper or card, about 60cm by 90cm. With a pencil, mark some roads on the card. Make an area for a park and another to put some houses and flats on. Now, paint the roads grey, and the gardens and park green.

To make the houses, trim boxes and cut some card to make the roofs. Paint the houses brick colour and add windows and doors. Paint the roofs grey and tape them on the houses. For flats, use a cereal box or two or three smaller boxes stuck on top of each other and paint lines across to look like windows and balconies.

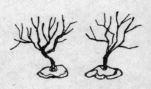

Use some of the boxes to make shops. Paint windows with signs above, saying 'Baker', 'Chemist', 'Supermarket'. Why not include a fire station, a hospital or a railway station?

Arrange your houses, shops and flats on the paper and make some trees from twigs stuck in plasticine. If you have any toy cars, trains or figures, then get them out. They will make your town look even more realistic.

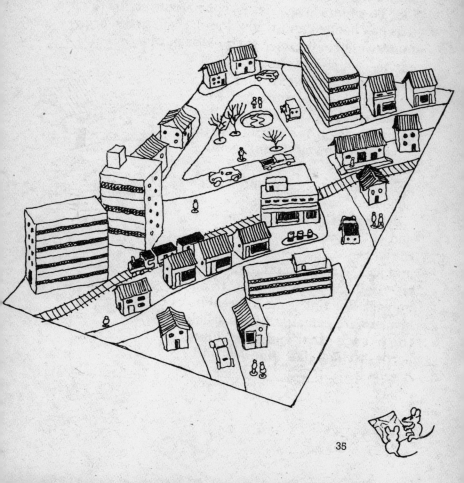

If you fancy **living in the country**, how about a little cottage near a farm? Use another large piece of paper or card, about 60cm by 90cm, and a piece of corrugated paper, about 30cm by 45cm. Cut the corrugated paper into field shapes and paint them; some green as grass or cabbages, some yellow for corn or wheat, and brown for a ploughed field. Don't forget to leave a space for the farm yard and for your cottage with its garden. Paint some narrow lanes leading from your cottage to the farmyard. You could even paint a little river winding its way across the countryside. To separate the fields, cut narrow strips of card to use as hedges and walls. Paint them green or grey and stick them in place with blobs of plasticine.

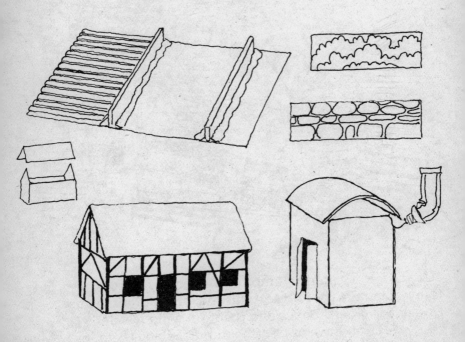

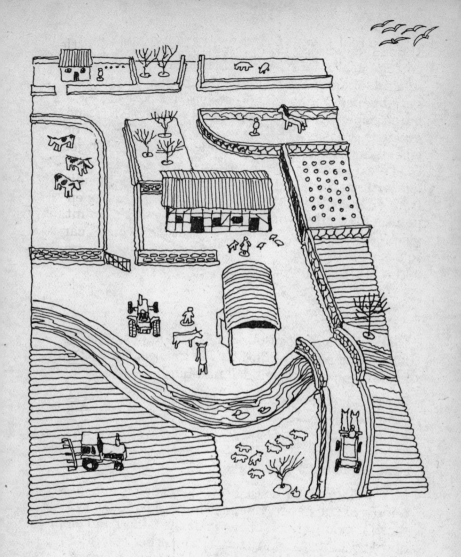

Use twigs stuck into lumps of plasticine as trees. Now, **to make the cottage** and the farm buildings, use small cardboard boxes and paint on windows and doors. If you have any farm animals, place them in the fields and farmyard.

If you really want to get away from it all, how about making a far away **tropical island**: here's how you do it . . .

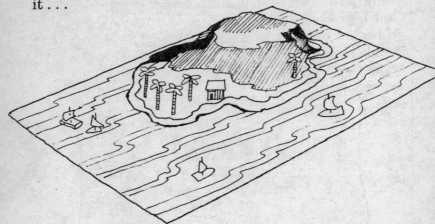

Find a large piece of paper or card, about 60cm by 90cm, and paint it blue. This is the sea. Now, for the island, you can use modelling dough.

For this you'll need:
6 cups of flour.
4 cups of salt
2 cups of water
8 tablespoons of cooking oil

Mix it all up in a plastic bowl then turn it out into the middle of the paper. Shape it into an island. Try to make a mountain on one side of the island and slope it down to a lovely sandy bay at the other side. Paint the island grey at the top of the mountain, green further down and finally, a lovely sandy coloured beach round the edge.
Use pipe cleaners painted green to make palm trees and stick them into the dough. A small box could make a beach hut

Hey, maybe this is a treasure island so you will need **a treasure map**. Get a square of paper and tear around the edges to make it look old. Hide a sweet or some little round pieces of card painted yellow like gold coins, on the island. Draw the shape of your island on the map and put an X to mark the spot where the treasure is hidden.

Fold it up and give it to a friend saying "X" marks the spot, and see if they can find the hidden treasure.

Now, if you feel like a change, you've got no problem. You have a choice of where to go . . . Happy roaming!

COME TO THE CIRCUS

I always gasp with amazement whenever I go the circus. It's such an exciting place! The trapeze artists, the jugglers, the tumbling acrobats and the funny clowns all make it a feast of fun.

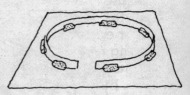

Why not make your own circus where your performers can have all the thrills and spills of the circus.

To make a circus ring you need a big piece of card painted brown for the base. Use long thin strips of card stuck together and bent into a circle to make the ring. Paint it bright colours and secure it to the base with lumps of plasticine.

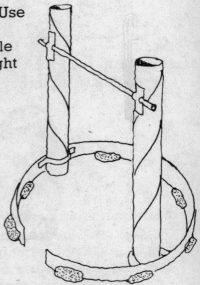

Paint two kitchen roll tubes with bright colours and stick them to the ring with tape. Tape a long stick between them for your trapeze artist to swing from.

I have found that match boxes make great performers. But please be careful only to use boxes when they're empty, please don't play with matches . . . Promise!

Now back to the circus . . . every circus has a daring **trapeze artist** so here's how to make one. Use an empty matchbox and paint it a bright colour. Paint the face on the back of the inside of the box. For the arms and legs push a pipe cleaner down each side and bend the hands over to hook on to the trapeze.

For the trapeze use a cocktail stick. Tie equal lengths of string or cotton thread to it and tie the other ends to the stick above your circus ring. Your daring trapeze artist is ready to perform. Now for the **tumbling acrobats**. Use the matchboxes, as before, but this time pile the boxes one on top of each other by pushing pipe cleaners down the sides. Use plasticine to make them stand up.

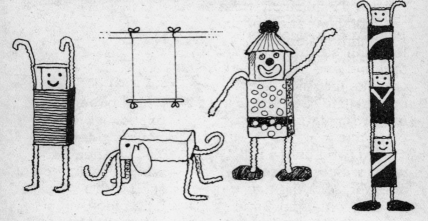

Make some crazy clowns again using empty matchboxes. Paint a clown's face complete with red nose and a hat cut from card.

Don't forget the performing **matchbox elephants** for the circus. Paint the box grey and use it flat this time. You will need three pipe cleaners, two for the legs and one for the trunk and tail. Cut out some ear shapes and attach them to the sides.

41

Now all your performers are ready to perform, so why don't you become the ringmaster? Haven't got an outfit? . . . Well, I'll show you how to make one.

First your **top hat** . . . you will need a piece of stiff paper long enough to go round your head. Paint it black, bend it into a tube and secure it with sticky tape.

Cut a circle of paper a little wider than the tube and cut a hole in it big enough to fit on your head. Paint it black too and tape it to the tube. Now you have a top hat.

For your **bow tie** cut the shape out of card and paint it with spots. To finish off, wear a red jacket, jumper or tee shirt and clip the bow tie to the front

with a paper clip or stick it on with double sided tape. You will need **a whip**. Use a piece of stick with a long piece of string attached to it. Now you're ready to announce the performers. "And now . . . Ladies and Gentlemen, Boys and Girls, welcome to 'The Matchbox Circus'!"

42

DINOSAURS

What are big? . . . What have strange names? . . . What do not exist any more? . . .
The answer is Dinosaurs.
Dinosaurs' names can be really strange tongue twisters like . . .
TRICERATOPS (Try-ser-a-tops)
TYRANNOSAURUS (Ti-ran-o-sor-us)
STEGOSAURUS (Steg-o-sor-us)
ORNITHOMIMUS (Or-nith-o-mim-us)
DIPLODOCUS (Dip-lo-doc-us)
BRACHIOSAURUS (Brak-i-o-sor-us)

You can be a dinosaur if you like, I'll show you how.
Get yourself a large box and cut it into this shape.
Take one of the side flaps and cut it into this shape.
Tape it on top of the box. String a few kitchen roll tubes together and attach them to the back of the box . . . this is the tail.
Paint the whole thing green with bright orange spots, or any colour you like. Now put the box on your back and get down on all fours.

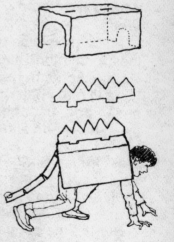

Before you start roaring and frightening everybody, think up a name for yourself ending in "saurus". Samanthasaurus, Petersaurus, Astisaurus, Wobbleasaurus, Boxasaurus.

Scrummy Tucks

I love eating and I'm always trying to think up delicious 'scrummy tucks' . . . my name for mouth-watering goodies.

Iced Sheep Dog

You need: *1 swiss roll, 1 litre block of ice cream, 8oz whipping cream or dream topping, 7 chocolate drops.*

Place the swiss roll on top of the ice cream block and cover it with whipped cream. Use a fork to make lines like the hair on an old English sheep dog. Use the choc drops as eyes, nose and a mouth.

West Indian Shave Ice

You need: *4 trays of ice cubes, 150ml strawberry or pineapple syrup, or orange juice, paper cups.*

Put the ice cubes in a clean tea towel and crush them a fine as possible (I use a rolling pin for this). Pack the ice into the cups and pour on the syrup.

My mum used to make this for me when I was little and I used to love it, in fact I still do! . . . Mmmm.

Bat's Blood

Blackcurrant juice and lemonade mixed together in a bottle labelled "Bat's Blood" . . . Try it on your friends . . . hee hee hee!

Calypso Cocktail

You need: *1 litre cream soda, juice of 2 lemons, 1 banana chopped, pineapple chunks, cherries.*

Mix all the ingredients together with crushed ice. Serve in tall glasses with straws.

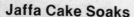

Jaffa Cake Soaks

You need: *½ packet of Jaffa Cakes, 4 tablespoons orange juice, Orange & Lemon sugared pieces, 2oz dream topping or whipped cream.*

Soak biscuits in juice sponge side up. Spread cream on top and decorate with orange and lemon pieces.

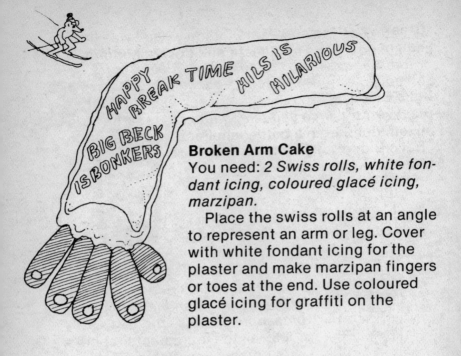

Broken Arm Cake

You need: *2 Swiss rolls, white fondant icing, coloured glacé icing, marzipan.*

Place the swiss rolls at an angle to represent an arm or leg. Cover with white fondant icing for the plaster and make marzipan fingers or toes at the end. Use coloured glacé icing for graffiti on the plaster.

Orange and Apple Ball

You need: *2 oranges, 2 apples.*

Cut apples and oranges into segments and re-shape into a ball using alternate pieces of apple and orange. Wrap in cling film until needed.

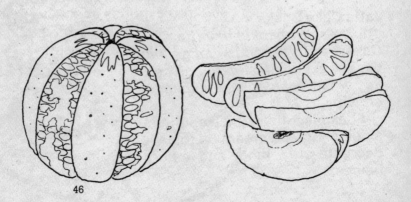

Greek Salad Sandwich

You need: *dash of lemon juice, chopped lettuce, 1 tomato (cubed), ¼ cucumber (cubed), 1 pitta bread, 2oz cheese (diced), 1 dessert spoon olive oil.*

Cut pitta bread in half and open each half into a pocket. Mix all the salad ingredients together and stir in the olive oil and lemon juice. Now put it into the pitta pockets . . . Yassos!

Sweet Mice

You need: *1lb icing sugar, 1 egg white (it's great fun separating an egg!), peanuts, liquorice sticks, silver sugar balls, 2 drops cochineal.*

Whisk the egg white then add sugar, cochineal and a little water if necessary. Make it firm enough to mould with the hands into a mouse shape. Give it peanut ears, silver ball eyes and cut liquorice sticks into strips and use them as tails. Leave to set.

Fun and Games

I love playing silly games, the sillier they are the better. How about these:

Whacky Ones

Tongue Tied. See if you can touch the end of your nose with your tongue. I have found very few people who can . . . are you one of them?

Ere Ere. Another whacky game is to try and look at your ears without a mirror.

Wiggy. Try to wiggle your ears. It's really funny watching people's faces while they're trying to do it.

Here are some zany tricks to try on your friends.

Untouchable. Ask them, "Where can your right hand go where your left hand can't reach it"? The answer is . . . On your left elbow.

Wally. Hold up two fingers and say "How many fingers am I **not** holding up"? They are bound to answer three and you say "What about the other hand, wally!"

Sticky Ball. Oh, this is a great zany trick to play on your friends. Screw up a piece of paper and wrap sticky tape around it sticky side out . . . this is a bit tricky, but it can be done. When you meet a friend casually say "catch" and throw them the ball. When they catch it, it will stick to them and they will find it difficult to throw it back!

Crisp Games

Crisps can be fun to eat. Here are three crisp eating games that will have you in stitches.

Shsh . . . Everyone sits facing each other with some crisps in front of them. The idea is to eat the crips without making a sound. It's not easy and it's hilarious.

Crunch! Sit facing each other again but this time eat the crisps as loudly as you can!

Chop Chop. This is my favourite . . . See who can eat crisps the fastest using chopsticks.

Wet Ones

Everyone knows that balloons are great fun to play with, but have you tried whacky summer water balloon games? Don't know any? Well here are a few. You will need to wear swimsuits or raincoats because you just might get wet. Interested? . . . Well, here comes the best bit. To play the games you need water filled-balloons!

A good tip is to only put a little water in the balloon then blow it up as normal.

Piggy in the Middle. Three people are needed for this game. The two end throwers have to throw the water-filled balloon to each other, and the one in the middle has to try to catch it, but beware! It could burst and you'll get soaked!

Knobbly Knees. Everyone lines up and on the word "go", they grab a water-filled balloon, put it between their knees and run as fast as they can for the finishing line.

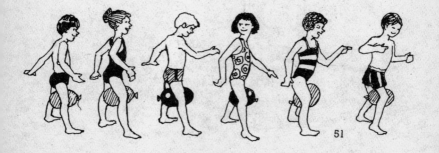

Water Fall. Everyone sits in two lines opposite each other. Toss a water-filled balloon in the air and the idea is to bat it over the head of the person opposite you, but it must not touch the ground.

Water Football. This can be great fun, trying to score goals with water-filled balloons. It's even greater fun if you try to score with a header!

Water Skittles. Here's a variation on that old favourite, skittles. Fill up six plastic bottles with water and stand them in a triangle pattern somewhere flat. (This game works best on the lawn.) Each player has a different coloured balloon. Fill the balloons with water then top them up with a few puffs of air.

The rest is simple. Each player rolls his or her balloon at the skittles and tries to knock them down. The trick is not to burst your balloon, otherwise you're out. The person who knocks over the most in five attempts, without bursting their balloon, is the winner.

Squirt. Are you a good squirt? Well now's your chance to find out. You will need two bowls, two empty washing up liquid bottles, a bucket and some pals. Fill the bucket with water and put it at one end of the garden. Put the bowls side by side at the other end.

Two of you arm yourselves with a washing up liquid bottle each and on the word "squirt", run to the bucket and fill up your bottle. Then run as fast as you can to your bowls and squirt like mad! The one who has squirted the most water into his or her bowl at the end of two minutes is the "Squirt of the Year".

Melt Down. This "wet one" is really silly and cold. You need ice cubes, a watch or clock with a second hand, and four or more pals. Choose one to be the referee and the rest all stand in a circle. The referee selects someone and gives him or her an ice cube which is then passed round the circle as fast as possible.

When the referee shouts "change" it has to be passed in the opposite direction. The person who is left with nothing to pass on, is out and so on until the winner is left. This person then has to see how long she or he can hold an ice cube before it melts, thus setting a record for the next game, the winner of which has to try to beat the record.

Had enough of being wet? . . . Well try some more dry **Whacky Ones:**

Limbo. Hang sweets, pieces of fruit or a biscut on a long stick and get two people to hold it a few feet off the ground. Now, try to "limbo" under it and bite off a sweet or piece of fruit as you go. The stick is lowered after each go to see who can limbo the lowest.

Atishoo. Here's a game that can be lots of fun. You need a few friends to play it. Each person has a drinking straw and she or he has to pick up a tissue by sucking through the straw and pass it to the next person. Anyone who drops it is out. Remember no hands!

Chin Chin. For this zany game you will need an orange and a few close friends, divided into two teams. The idea is to hold the orange under your chin and pass it to the next person who has to take it under his or her chin . . . No hands please.

The first team to drop the orange loses.

Me and My Dog. This game is like a sheepdog trial. Set an obstacle course around the garden e.g chairs, a bucket of water, a tunnel made from a floor rug etc. Now you need teams of two, one person is the shepherd and the other is the dog. Here comes the zany bit . . . the dog has to be blindfolded and the shepherd has to guide the dog through the obstacle course by shouting out instructions such as "left", or "right", "forward", "back" and so on. The idea is to see which team can get around the course in the fastest time without knocking over any of the obstacles.

Double Blind Man's Buff. If you like playing blind man's buff then try it the zany way. You need eight people or more but you must have even numbers. Everyone chooses a partner and ties one leg to the partner's leg, as they would for a three-legged race. One team is then blindfolded and has to try to catch another team. It's hilarious!

Time's Up. For this you need an alarm clock, a small cardboard box and a few pals. Set the alarm clock to go off in two or three minutes. The person who is "it" holds the box and has to chase and touch one of the others who then has to take the box, and so it goes on until the alarm goes off. If you are holding the box when the alarm goes off, your time's up and you are out!

Dizzy. This is a real whacky game which I have never been able to do, but it's fun trying. Hold up a pole above your head and spin round fifteen times. Now drop the pole and see if you can jump over it!

This is not for those who suffer from sea sickness.

Errgh! Dare you put your hand in a large tub full of torn up paper mixed with water, wood shavings and wall paper paste and a bit of green powder paint to find the treasure? This revolting game is great fun to play. The treasure could be 5p or 10p pieces, but mixed in can be duds, like bottle tops. This makes it more exciting. Each hunter has thirty seconds to feel for the treasure if they dare!

Fun Jewellery

I love wearing fun jewellery. It always makes people smile and it makes me feel happy. It's great fun to make too! So I'll tell you how to make some of my favourite jewellery.

Polo Necklace. You need a packet of polos and some coloured wool. Cut the wool into small pieces and loop each piece around a polo. Tie it together to form a chain. Don't forget to leave enough wool at the ends to secure it around your neck.

Fruity Necklace. You need a packet of fruit polos, some pieces of coloured wool and some clear nail polish to seal the surface of the sweets. Paint the polos with the nail polish and when they are dry, loop them together with the wool to form a chain. Now you have a colourful necklace.

Macaroni Necklace and Bangle. Use large macaroni pieces (make sure they have big holes through the middle). Use felt-tip pens to colour the pieces and then thread them on to a piece of string or wool. Now you have a unique necklace. Make a smaller one to wear as a bangle.

57

Sparkling Necklace and Bracelet. Roll up small balls of silver foil. Then use a darning needle to make holes through the balls. Thread them on to a piece of string. Make a large one as the necklace and a smaller one as a bracelet. There! you have a sparkling fun set to wear at parties.

Cotton Reel Necklace. Use very small reels of cotton of different colours. Thread them on to a piece of thin ribbon and you'll have a necklace with a difference.

Star Badge. Cut out a picture of your favourite pop or TV star and stick it on to a circle of stiff card. Cover it with cling film. Tape a safety pin on the back so you can attach it to your jacket.

Glitter Badge. Cut out a circle of card, paint it a bright colour. Let it dry then coat it with glue and sprinkle it with glitter powder. Cover it with cling film. Tape a safety pin on the back and there you have a glittering badge.

58

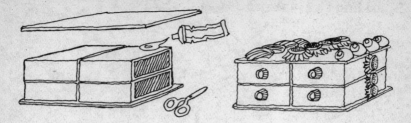

You will need some thing to put your jewellery in. So here's how to make a simple **jewellery box**.

You need four jumbo size match boxes, some stiff card and four toothpaste tube tops. Stick the boxes together like this and paint them. Cut out two pieces of card to cover the top and bottom of the boxes. Stick them on with glue then paint them, and decorate them with shells or dried flowers. Stick the toothpaste tube tops on to each drawer.

Now you have a very special jewellery box.

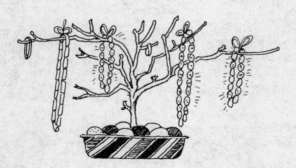

You could also **make a trinket tree**.

Find a small twig with as many branches as possible. Paint it, and push it into a lump of plasticine at the bottom of an empty plastic margarine tub that has been painted or covered with foil. Find some nice round pebbles to fill up the rest of the tub.

Now you can hang your unique fun jewellery on the branches of your trinket tree.

PARTY TIME

Yippee, it's party time!

If you want your party to be a bit special I'll tell you a few ways to do just that.

It all starts with the invitations. It's always a good idea to have a theme for your party and make the invitations to suit.

If you're having a horror party, send out invitations in the shape of a bat cut from black card and use a white pencil to write on them.

Or have a pirate party; the invitations could be made to look like a treasure map.

For a pop star or TV star party, cut out star shapes and stick glitter around the edges.

Have a space party; the invitations could be in the shape of a rocket.

How about a fairy tale party? Use the shape of an open book and write the invitation on the pages.

Ever thought of having a sporty party? This time, use the shape of the olympic rings for your invite.

A good way to set the mood of your party is to **decorate the room**. I always cut out big letter shapes from old wrapping paper to spell out "Happy Birthday" or "Welcome!" Then I hang them on the wall and festoon them with balloons and streamers.

Stick a few balloons outside the
front door to help your guests find the
party.

Fancy Dress . . . Wowee!

I think the best part of the party is
the dressing up bit, especially when it's
for fancy dress parties. Make the cos-
tumes out of paper, old bits of material
or old clothes. Use face paints and make-up to complete
your character. (Use non-toxic paints mixed with baby
lotion for your face).

If you can't think what to wear for your party, here are a
few ideas: For a **horror party**, paint your face green or
purple for starters, and wear a white sheet or a witch's hat
(see page 16) or dress up as a Ghostbuster. Wear a white tee-
shirt or track suit and carry a haversack on your back and a
ghost blaster! (A water pistol will do.)

For the **pirates' party**, cut out a pirate's hat from black stiff
paper or use a piece of material as a headscarf. Finish off
with a big round earring. Lick a tiny square of black paper
and press it on to one of your front teeth to black it out.

Draw a treasure map and carry it around with you. Say to
everyone you meet, "Ah, Jim lad, X marks the spot where
the treasure's buried."

For a **pop star** or **TV star party** choose your favourite star and try to look like her or him by wearing make up, dark glasses, beads, hats, long plaits made from coloured wool. You could even dress up as a super hero; wear a blue leotard, red underpants and a paper cape.

For a **space party** dress up in a spaceman's outfit (see page 20) or be an alien. For this, use face paint to make your face look as weird as possible. Draw on an extra eye or spray your hair with a wash off colour spray. The weirder you look the better.

For a **fairy tale party** there are so many characters to dress as. Be Red Hiding Hood . . . you will need a red cape and hood though, so make it from a long sheet of crepe paper. Fold it in half and stick one edge together. Cut a triangle out from the other edge and fold back the front edges of the hood.

To keep it on cut a long strip of crepe paper and tie it loosely round your neck. To finish off carry a basket with some goodies in it for Granny.

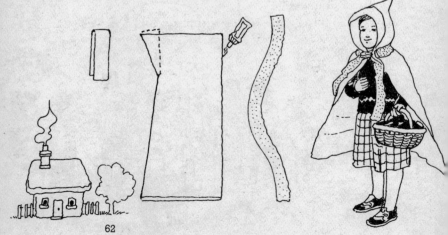

Or be Humpty Dumpty . . . wear a track suit and stick cushions down the trousers and up the front to look like a big round egg.

For a **sporty party** you can dress up to play your favourite sport. Be an athlete, wear a track suit or shorts and vest with a number pinned on to it. Other sporty ideas could be a jockey, a snooker player or a BMX rider. Be a tennis player . . . carry a racket cut out of card and wear shorts, a tee-shirt and trainers. Go round saying "You cannot be serious!"

Or you could just wear jewellery you have made.

To entertain your party guests try out some of the magic tricks (page 23) and games (page 48) I've shown you. I hope you've been practising!

Hey! Try making some of my scrummy tucks as well!

Happy party time!

I hope you've enjoyed all the ways I have thought up for you to have fun. I had a great time thinking them up and I'm working on another 101 ways for you to have fun.

    Enjoy yourselves . . . bye for now.

    Love and hugs, Floella.